Holy Week at Home

*Adaptations of the Palm Sunday,
Holy Thursday, Good Friday,
Easter Vigil, and Easter Sunday Rituals
for Family and Household Prayer*

John T. Kyler

*These prayers are not intended to replace the liturgies of Holy Week.
Rather, they are a sincere effort to cultivate some of the rituals and
spirit of Holy Week in our own homes when public celebration
might not be possible.*

LITURGICAL PRESS
Collegeville, Minnesota

www.litpress.org

For Christine Rojek
and the people of Most Holy Redeemer Parish,
Evergreen Park, Illinois,
who instilled in me a love for liturgy

Cover design by Tara Wiese.

ISBN 978-0-8146-6666-1   978-0-8146-6667-8 (e-book)

Palm Sunday of the Lord's Passion

Introduction

Palm Sunday celebrates two seemingly different stories. We begin the liturgy by commemorating Jesus's triumphant journey to Jerusalem where he is greeted by shouts and songs of acclamation and joy. Everything seems to be going well. Jesus is hailed as a King and people wave palm branches to show their honor for him. By the time we reach the Gospel, however, we hear the Passion of Jesus Christ, recalling the events leading up to his crucifixion and death on the cross. It may seem strange that these two extremes are celebrated on Palm Sunday, but that is the reality of the paschal mystery. There is only one story. Jesus' life, death and resurrection are all connected; it is impossible to separate them as isolated events. The same is true for our lives. Everything we do is united with Christ, the good times and the difficult ones. Even when God seems distant and far away, we know that we are always connected to the story of Jesus's life, death and resurrection. We are always connected to Christ.

As we begin Holy Week, take a moment to recall this narrative of Christ with your family. What are some events from Jesus' life that stand out to you? Do you have a favorite parable or story of healing? It is important to remember that the Jesus who walked and taught and ate is the same Jesus who dies and rises again. Think too about your own life. What are some of the significant events you have experienced this past year? Recall some of these moments aloud as you continue to share the story of your family, which is also the story of Christ!

Ritual at Home

Perhaps the most memorable part of the Palm Sunday liturgy is the Commemoration of the Lord's Entrance into Jerusalem. To help us celebrate, the church invites us to carry palm branches as we gather for prayer today. Even so, we remember that liturgy is not a recreation of past events. Rather, it is *anamnesis*, an active remembering of the past so that we may live those realities today.

Opening Prayer:
Loving God,
As we come to the beginning of Holy Week,
we remember your triumphant entry into Jerusalem.
We sing your praises, shouting, "Hosanna to the Son
    of David."
You alone are the true King, the leader greater than
    all others.
Even so, in your great mercy you chose to become like us,
taking on human form and living among us.
As we celebrate and shout "Hosanna" today,
may we remember what will soon follow.
Keep us faithful in word and deed,
and help us love you to the best of our ability.

We ask this through Christ, our Lord. Amen.

Reading: Matthew 21:1-11

Procession:
We, too, welcome Jesus, the Son of David,
the one who comes in the name of the Lord,
the King of Israel.
Holding our palm branches, let us acclaim Christ,
    the Lord.

If circumstances allow, a short procession around the house (inside or outside!) would be appropriate, with all responding, "Hosanna to the Son of David!" Children may wish to make banners or streamers to wave in the procession and play tambourines or other percussion instruments. You can use palms from last year that you might still have, other tree leaves, or even homemade crafted leaves.

To Jesus, the True Light, who illumines the darkness and brings us hope during difficult times.
Hosanna to the Son of David!

To Jesus, the Prince of Peace, who models compassion and inclusion, sensitivity and goodwill.
Hosanna to the Son of David!

To Jesus, the Master Teacher, who shows by example how to accompany others, offering gentle guidance and direction.
Hosanna to the Son of David!

To Jesus, the Great Healer, who cares for the sick with tenderness and mercy, showing love to heal body, mind, and spirit.
Hosanna to the Son of David!

To Jesus, the Paschal Victim, who dies so that we might rise to new life.
Hosanna to the Son of David!

Intercessions:
Confident that Jesus Christ hears our prayer,
let us offer our petitions with open hearts.

For the Pope, and all church leaders: May they continue to boldly lead, offering prophetic witness to the Gospel.

For all people in positions of leadership: May they work tirelessly for peace and justice to ensure the common good for all.

For all families and communities, especially those longing for intimacy and communion: May they know the tenderness of compassion and the joy of inclusion.

For our own needs this day: *Prayers may be offered aloud.*

For all who have died: May they rest and rise in Christ.

The Lord's Prayer:
Gathering these prayers together,
as well as those we hold in the silence of our hearts,
we pray in the words that Jesus taught us.

Our Father . . .

Prayer:
Loving God,
We praise you in a special way today as we celebrate
    Palm Sunday.
Be with us as we begin our journey through Holy Week,
that we may more closely align our lives with yours,
knowing suffering and death,
yet remaining hopeful in the life you promise.

We ask this through Christ, our Lord. Amen.

All are invited to share a sign of Christ's peace.

Conversation Starters
1. What images, words, or phrases do you associate with Palm Sunday?
2. The Palm Sunday liturgy shows the fickleness of humanity. One minute we shout someone's praises, and soon after we yell, "Crucify him!" When in your own life have you been inconsistent in your actions or beliefs?
3. What is your prayer as you begin Holy Week?

Continuing the Conversation

The *Rule of Saint Benedict* encourages us to welcome all as Christ. With this, we are called to see and welcome Jesus in all whom we encounter. As we celebrate Jesus's entry into Jerusalem and hear of the people who welcomed him, think about the ways your own family welcomes Jesus through the people who visit your home. Work together to create a sign to hang near your door, reminding you to "Welcome all as Christ."

Thursday of the Lord's Supper
(Holy Thursday)

Introduction

The Sacred Paschal Triduum begins with the Evening Mass of the Lord's Supper on Holy Thursday. The word *Triduum* comes from the Latin for "three days." These three days of Holy Thursday, Good Friday, and the Easter Vigil/Easter Sunday are the highpoint of our entire liturgical year. Holy Thursday especially commemorates Jesus' command to serve others, modeled explicitly in the washing of feet and the celebration of the Eucharist. How do you serve others in your own family and community? Why is it important to connect our daily service to others with Jesus's command to do so?

Even when we are unable to gather to celebrate Eucharist, we are still called to be a eucharistic people. Jesus's self-gift in the Eucharist allows us to give freely of ourselves to others, following Jesus's instructions, "Do this in memory of me." Our own table fellowship with our family and friends is also a participation in the Eucharist, because the Eucharist by its very nature is deeply relational. If we limit our understanding of Eucharist to only what we receive at Mass, we are missing a major part of Christ's invitation to us. "Do this in memory of me" is a command and call to action. Do we dare to live our lives following the example of Christ?

Ritual at Home

The *pedilavium*, or foot washing, has been a Holy Thursday practice for centuries. A concrete representation of our call to service, the foot washing in the Holy Thursday liturgy reminds us of Jesus' example and command. If we truly understand this command, however, we realize that we are called to do more than literally wash feet. This is a ritual that reminds us of our call to serve others through the concrete realities of life.

Opening Prayer:
Loving God,
You show us by example how to love others.
Today as we celebrate Holy Thursday,
we remember when you washed the feet of your disciples.
Give us the strength to wash each other's feet,
not only in the ritual moment of today,
but in all moments of our lives.
May we as a family recommit ourselves to the service
of others.

We ask this through Christ, our Lord. Amen.

Reading: John 13:1-15

Washing of Feet:
Placing a pitcher of warm water, a large bowl, and a towel in front of those gathered, one of the adults might invite everyone to sit in a circle on the ground.

A designated leader reads:
We follow Jesus' example and celebrate our own washing of feet. Throughout our time together, pay close attention to what you are experiencing and how you feel.

I now invite you to slowly remove your shoes and socks. What do you feel? How do you think Jesus's friends must have felt as they were preparing for him to wash their feet? What do you imagine Jesus was thinking as he began washing?

The leader takes the feet of one person and places them in the bowl. Pouring some water over the feet, and looking the person in the eye, the leader says:

If washing feet with children:
(Name), I love you. Be kind to one another, help each other, and love everyone you meet.

If washing feet with only adults:
(Name), I love you and Christ loves you. Share the love of Christ with everyone you meet.

One person may wash the feet of all present or each person may take a turn, washing the feet of their neighbor after their own feet have been washed. After washing each person's feet, gently dry their feet with the towel.

Intercessions:
Confident that Jesus Christ hears our prayer,
let us offer our petitions with open hearts.

For all who serve in our church: May they follow the example of Christ and uphold the dignity of all people.

For all who serve in our community and country: May they work for the good of all people, especially people who are poor and relegated to the margins of society.

For all who serve others every day, especially parents, guardians, teachers, coaches, and all who practice selflessness and self-gift: May they find comfort and hope knowing that their actions make a difference to so many.

For all gathered here: May we live lives of service to God and others, even when it is difficult or requires extra effort.

The Lord's Prayer:
Gathering these prayers together,

as well as those we hold in the silence of our hearts,
we pray in the words that Jesus taught us.

Our Father . . .

Prayer:
Loving God,
We praise you in a special way today as we celebrate
     Holy Thursday.
Be with us as we continue our journey through Holy Week,
that we may more closely align our lives with yours,
knowing our call to serve others
following the example you gave.

We ask this through Christ, our Lord. Amen.

All are invited to share a sign of Christ's peace.

Conversation Starters
1. What images, words, or phrases do you associate with Holy Thursday?
2. How does Jesus call you to serve others in your everyday actions and interactions?
3. How might you explain the connection between the washing of feet and Eucharist?

Continuing the Conversation
The Eucharist is rooted in community and table fellowship. What does table fellowship look like in your own home? What are some ways you can commit or recommit to the sharing of family meals? Perhaps today would be a good opportunity to cook and eat dinner together. Each family member can take on a specific role, from cooking, to setting the table, to washing the dishes. It is in spending time together that we can live the "thanksgiving" at the heart of Eucharist.

Friday of the Passion of the Lord (Good Friday)

Introduction

As we celebrate the Passion of Jesus Christ and hear John's Gospel account of his suffering and death, we are reminded of the injustices that pervade our world. Often these systems of oppression, hate, and fear are so commonplace that we do not even notice them. Good Friday serves as a good reminder of this reality. It is easy to become discouraged, to see the work that has to be done and look away. Today we pray that we may have the conscience to see and the courage to act, remembering that death never wins. Life and love always prevail in Christ.

The traditional Good Friday liturgy contains three unique components: the reading of John's Passion, the praying of The Solemn Intercessions, and the Adoration of the Holy Cross. Each of these helps us enter more fully into our relationship with Christ and recommits us to pray and work for the good of the church and world.

Ritual at Home

The Adoration of the Holy Cross begins with a Showing of the Holy Cross. While there are two options for this ritual, unveiling the cross or processing the cross through church, both forms include a sung proclamation: Behold, the wood of the Cross. The rubrics for the Adoration of the Cross call for a cross rather than a crucifix, as it highlights the major symbol of the crucified and risen Christ. Rather than an act of idolatry, the Adoration of the Cross points us to the Risen Christ.

While the Good Friday liturgy calls for a cross sans *corpus*, your home adaptation might use a crucifix, if that is what you have.

Opening Prayer:
Lord of Glory,
we proclaim your death and look ever forward to your
    Resurrection.
As we contemplate your cross,
the tree on which you hung so that we may have life,
may we be ever aware of the life that springs from death,
the light that rises from darkness,
and the hope that banishes fear.
Draw us close to you,
so that we may know the glory
your cross points to.

We ask this through Christ, our Lord. Amen.

Reading: John 18:1–19:42

Adoration of the Cross:
Place a cross on a table or some other place of honor, adding candles if you wish. Be sure to allow some time in silent reflection as you gaze upon the cross and grow in relationship with Jesus.

Part of the beauty of the Adoration of the Cross is the time for personal prayer and reflection, as well as performing individual acts of reverence. You may wish to touch the cross, or show another suitable sign, such as genuflection or a kiss. Do not let this time be cluttered by words but bask in the power of the cross as a symbol of not only death but ultimately of Resurrection.

To begin and end the time of reflection, simply proclaim and respond: Behold, the wood of the Cross.

At some point during the period of reflection, you may wish to pray the following Litany for Forgiveness.

Litany for Forgiveness:

For the times we have not loved as we are called to love . . .
Father, forgive.

For the times we have cultivated doubt instead of hope . . .
Father, forgive.

For the times that selfishness, greed, and lust influence our decisions . . .
Father, forgive.

For the times we nurture isolation instead of community . . .
Father, forgive.

For the times we hear the needs of others but refuse to act . . .
Father, forgive.

For the times we pass judgment on ourselves and those whom we encounter . . .
Father, forgive.

For the times we create divisions . . .
Father, forgive.

For the times we neglect care for our common home . . .
Father, forgive.

For the times we are not good stewards of the gifts you give us . . .
Father, forgive.

Intercessions:

Confident that Jesus Christ hears our prayer,
let us offer our petitions with open hearts.

For the church, for the Pope, and for all women and men
who live their lives in service of God: May they know the
intimacy of authentic relationship with Christ.

For catechumens and for all who are preparing to celebrate
sacraments: May they respond to their baptismal call with
courage, opening their hearts to the invitation of God.

For all who are sick or suffering in body, mind, or spirit: May
they know the great compassion of God through those who
care for them.

For peace in our families, communities, nation, and world:
May all seek resolution to disagreement and difference in
ways that protect the life and dignity of all people.

For all who are unemployed or underemployed: May they
find opportunities to use their gifts for the service of others
in ways that are sustaining and life-giving.

For all who grieve: May they know the consolation of hope
found in Christ.

The Lord's Prayer:

Gathering these prayers together,
as well as those we hold in the silence of our hearts,
we pray in the words that Jesus taught us.

Our Father . . .

Prayer:

Loving God,

We praise you in a special way today as we celebrate
    Good Friday.

Be with us as we continue our journey through Holy Week,
that we may more closely align our lives with yours,
knowing that death never wins,
and that life and love always prevail.

We ask this through Christ, our Lord. Amen.

All are invited to share a sign of Christ's peace.

Conversation Starters

1. What images, words, or phrases do you associate with
   Good Friday?
2. What are your own experiences of death and resurrection?
3. How might you explain the significance of the cross to
   someone?

Continuing the Conversation

Take some time to pray the prescribed psalm from today's
liturgy. Psalm 31 is a beautiful testimony of trust in God.

The Easter Vigil in the Holy Night (Holy Saturday)

Introduction

"Exult, let them exult!" We hear these words at the beginning of the *Exsultet*, The Easter Proclamation, as we trace God's saving action throughout history. The name *Exsultet* comes from the first word of the prayer: Exult! As a Christian people we do exult, for Christ is risen from the dead and light banishes all traces of darkness.

The Easter Vigil liturgy is rich with symbol and ritual, and the Scripture readings connect us to our ancestors in faith, living the very same hope that we live today. The Genesis reading highlights God's incredible work of creation, and reminds us that creation and recreation continue today. Abraham's sacrifice recalls God's promises and abundant blessings for God's people, just as the reading from Exodus in which the Israelites cross the Red Sea prefigures Christ's own resurrection. Readings from the prophets follow, those great heralds of God's message throughout the ages. The Epistle from Paul to the Romans reinforces our baptismal identity and relationship with Jesus Christ who died and rose.

If time permits, read each of these Scripture passages in your own commemoration of The Easter Vigil. Each of these stories highlights God's love for God's people and helps us to celebrate Christ's resurrection by recalling God's saving action.

Ritual at Home

The rubrics for The Easter Vigil clearly state that the celebration must take place in the night and end before dawn, for the contrasts between darkness and light are essential. The celebration begins with *Lucernarium*, a service of light often associated with the early church tradition of lighting lamps for evening prayer and rejoicing in the light of Christ.

As you prepare an area for tonight's prayer, you may wish to light a number of candles. If possible, each person might also have their own candle to hold.

Opening Prayer:

We gather this night to rejoice in Jesus Christ, the Light of
    the World,
the One whom no darkness can overcome,
the One death cannot destroy.

Lighting the candles, continue:

We give you thanks, O God,
for the light this evening that illumines our hearts and home,
and for your Son, our Lord, Jesus Christ,
a light so filled with glory and power,
a light undimmed by sin and death,
a light that guides peoples and nations.

May we welcome this light of Christ into our lives. Amen.

Proclamation:

All respond: Thanks be to God!

This is the night when Christ poured out his own blood, cleansing us of the ancient sin of Adam: *Thanks be to God!*

This is the night when the Paschal Lamb was slain, anointing the hearts and homes of believers: *Thanks be to God!*

This is the night when Moses led the Israelites out of slavery in Egypt through the Red Sea: *Thanks be to God!*

This is the night when Christ rose from the dead, banishing death and darkness forever: *Thanks be to God!*

Thanks be to God!: *Thanks be to God!*

Reading: Matthew 28:1-10

Litany of the Saints:
Typically, this is the night when catechumens who have been preparing for Initiation are baptized. We pray for all catechumens, that they may know the joy of the Risen Christ as the source of their Christian identity. *If you know the catechumens from your parish, feel free to pray for them by name.*

As is also customary, we call on the intercession of those holy women and men who have walked before us and whose example guides us today. After each invocation, the response is: Pray for us. This list of saints is by no means comprehensive. Add your own favorite saints to the litany!

Holy Mary, Mother of God: *Pray for us.*
Saint Joseph: *Pray for us.*
Saint John the Baptist: *Pray for us.*
Saint Peter and Saint Paul: *Pray for us.*
Saint Mary Magdalene: *Pray for us.*
Saint Felicity and Saint Perpetua: *Pray for us.*
Saint Benedict and Saint Scholastica: *Pray for us.*
All holy men and women: *Pray for us.*

Intercessions:
All are welcome to share their own prayers, with everyone responding: "Risen Christ, Light and Life, hear our prayer."

The Lord's Prayer:
Gathering these prayers together,
as well as those we hold in the silence of our hearts,
we pray in the words that Jesus taught us.

Our Father . . .

Prayer:
Loving God,
We celebrate your saving work
through our ancestors in faith,
the Resurrection of your Son,
and in our own lives today.
Give us the courage to confront the darkness of this world,
knowing that the Risen Christ brings light and life to all.

We ask this through Christ, our Lord. Amen.

All are invited to share a sign of Christ's peace.

Conversation Starters
1. What images, words, or phrases do you associate with Holy Saturday?
2. Which Easter Vigil reading from Hebrew Scripture is your favorite? Why?
3. What role do you play in salvation history?

Continuing the Conversation
Reach out to the catechumens in your community. Perhaps you can send them a card or e-mail to let them know that you are thinking about and praying for them during this Easter season. Send these notes of care to the parish office or Director of Faith Formation so that they can share them with the catechumens. It is important that our faith communities actively support our catechumens!

The Resurrection of the Lord (Easter Sunday)

Introduction
Christ is risen! Alleluia! When we read today's Gospel it is easy for us to laugh at Mary of Magdala. How could she not have known that Jesus had risen? Sometimes we have to remind ourselves that we know how the story goes. Imagine the utter shock of visiting the tomb of a loved one to find it empty. John's Gospel notes that even Simon Peter and the disciple whom Jesus loved did not understand what had happened. Perhaps this is an invitation for each of us to think deeply about what the Resurrection means in our own lives.

Ritual at Home
The Easter Sunday liturgy celebrates Resurrection through the lens of discipleship. We hear the Gospel story of Mary and the disciples running to the tomb and reflect on the urgency of living our own baptismal call.

Create a prayer space full of greenery and flowers. On a table that is easy accessible by everyone, place a bowl of holy water.

Opening Prayer:
Loving God,
We celebrate this day of gladness and rejoicing,
basking in the depth of your love
revealed in an empty tomb.
May we, like the disciples, make haste
to share the news of Resurrection with everyone
we encounter.

We ask this through Christ, our Lord. Amen.

Reading: John 20:1-9

After an extended period of silent reflection, each person is welcome to sign themselves with the holy water, recalling the waters of Baptism and our commitment to life in Christ. You might wish to play some soft, instrumental music in the background during this ritual signing. You may also wish to proclaim the Apostles' Creed together to conclude this ritual moment.

Intercessions:
Confident that the living God is truly present in our lives, we raise our petitions, confident that they will be heard.

For the Pope and all church leaders: May they guide the faithful with the patience and kindness the Risen Christ shows to the disciples.

For all who support and nurture life, especially healthcare workers, teachers, and public servants: May they find joy in their vocation of service to others.

For all who celebrate new beginnings this Easter season: May they know life and love in their experiences and opportunities.

For all who work for equality and justice: May they never tire of proclaiming the peace of Christ.

For all who are sad or suffering during this time of Easter Alleluias: May they find the consolation of Christ through all those who love and support them.

The Lord's Prayer:
Gathering these prayers together,
as well as those we hold in the silence of our hearts,
we pray in the words that Jesus taught us.

Our Father . . .

Prayer:
Loving God,
We celebrate the life and love that you proclaim and share
    with us.
May we know the joy of your Resurrection in our hearts
as we strive to share this joy with others.
Like Mary, Simon Peter and the beloved disciple,
may we run to spread the Good News of the life and love
    you share.

We ask this through Christ, our Lord. Amen.

All are invited to share a sign of Christ's peace.

Conversation Starters
1. What images, words, or phrases do you associate with Easter Sunday?
2. What are some important Easter traditions in your own family?
3. Where do you encounter the Risen Christ?

Continuing the Conversation

As you celebrate the Easter season, take time to notice the daily experiences of resurrection and new life. Share these moments with your family and friends at the end of each day or week. You might be surprised how much new life permeates our world!